PETER SCHUMANN

FAUST 3

Copyright © 2016 by Peter Schumann

All rights reserved. No part of this book may be reproduced in any form or by any means without the prior written consent, except in the case of brief quotations used in reviews and certain other noncommercial uses permitted by copyright law.

ISBN-13: 978-1-942515-55-5
Library of Congress Control Number: 2016943572

Fomite
58 Peru Street
Burlington, VT 05401
www.fomitepress.com

PETER SCHUMANN

FAUST 3

In a recent clandestine interview at his graveside, Goethe was asked whether Faust's search for meaning he had committed his life to was completed by the end of Faust 2, or whether this search should be resumed. Goethe said : we now very definitely need Faust 3.

When our kids were little we regularly took them to the Black Forest to visit my parents & hike to the nearby ruins of the Stauffen castle, where the historic Faust had been employed as court magician & alchemist & where he signed his contract with the devil.

When Goethe died at age 82, his last words were: more light! I, Pe Schu, 82, sourdough rye baker, feel obliged to continue Goethe's quest for more light, obliged to tell him where to find the More of the light he requested, right there, near Faust's residence by the side of the Black Forest, on the other side of the Rhine, in Alsace, the most ecstatic light ever painted in the history of painting, the Isenheim altar by Mathias Grünewald, arising from the deepest darkness of the terrifying doomsday event: the solar eclipse of 1502 .

Antonine monks ran a hospital in Isenheim to treat victims of St. Anthony's fire, one of the most awful diseases of the middle age, caused by ergot, a rye-mold & so especially devastating to a rye-bread-eating population.

During the peasant wars in the early 16th century the Antonine monks commissioned the engineer, painter & peasant-war sympathizer Mathias Grünewald to paint an altar to address the terrible wounds that the rye mold had caused. One panel of the altar depicts the patron saint's martyrdom. The order was in possession of the saint's bones, which the monks used to brew an elixir, which, when used in the presence of Grünewald's altar, was to heal the sufferers. But even more: the demons that Grünewald painted to demonstrate the severity of St. Anthony's temptations - looking very much like ergot-induced hallucinations - found their way out of the hospital into the common life: flying straight from the altar onto the grist mills that grind grain in the Black Forest and in Alsace. Mounted to the mouths of the mills were wood-carved "flour-pukers", whose task was to frighten the rye mold away from the rye berries.

Goethe died after he completed Faust 2 & according to the faithful chronicler of his later years, Eckermann, expressed satisfaction, not only with Faust 2 but with the total of his life's work - the exact same satisfaction that killed the protagonist of Faust 2 because it fulfilled in precise words Faust's contract with the devil:

Zum Augenblicke dürft' ich sagen:
Verweile doch, du bist so schön!
Es kann die Spur von meinen Erdentagen
Nicht in Aeonen untergehn.

To this beautiful moment I will say
please linger on, don't go away!
The trace of all that my life employed
can't vanish in the eternal void. (PS trans.)

Goethe's more-light request is the generic quest of an overlit civilization.

In a culture where seeing is an industry more than human talent, & hearing a business more than ability of the heart & the mind itself, a negotiable uncertainty, not a wind or a storm which can toss reality off its pedestal in order to be real, the more-light issue is of no particular interest -- ah! Unless interest is revolutionized!

Pe Schu

Scene 1

THE GRISTMILL

Faust: I, Faust, formerly a complete life & an opposition to the existing form of life, eventually satisfied & therefore buried, then extracted from the grave by both heaven & hell for their specific purposes – am now obliged to be regurgitated back into life, to reconstruct myself according to modern measurement & need – in order to oversee the invention & retardation of progress – to disseminate the fog that hides the unbearable facts as well as to exercise the muscles of light, with which to fight the unbearable. This time my dissatisfaction with the status quo will need 2 guides & accomplices, devil & angel, whom you may or may not recognize in their undercover agent uniforms, but whose presence will be felt intensely throughout the proceedings.

If you can't figure out the connection between the forthcoming scenes: that's o.k., because the main thrust of my new job is provocation & confusion. The first task of my new being means exactly this: the disordering of the existing order of life as it inhabits the earth, our chthonic mother and our own soul's keeper & functioner.

a) angel & devil churn traditional Black Forest grist mill with demon face. Rye is milled into flour bag
b) when they turn the flour bag upside down the Faust 3 doll falls from it
c) they place the doll on a dollhouse chair next to desk with book
d) angel & devil change into their undercover agent uniforms
e) they then recite the bump bump verses

And now listen to this, to the deprived soul's functioning song:

> Bump bump bump
> We are in a slump
> where oh where is the heaven gone
> that our arts have painted for so long?
> the wind blows in the winter chills
> we live in order to pay the bills.
> the sun shines bright
> but we lack light
> the moon is beautiful
> but we are dutiful
> members of our civilization
> unrelated to our vocation
> half sick half jolly
> sucked into totalitarian folly

Scene 2

INCOMPETENT CHILDREN

The masses enter, fall, get up, push forward, down & up till dark, darkness produces dark masses chorale, moon is brought, masses reposition themselves according to moon location, moon orchestra performs, insufficiently though, masses push it away. Sun is brought in. 1. undercover agent directs police to channel the crowd & divide them up. 2. undercover agent sneaks out several individuals and hides them.

cops: This way, no, I mean that way, forward, upward, underward, go, stop, go, not now, can I, no you can't, any question, keep moving, over here, not yet, please, no *(a door is brought)*
line up, here, not here
(some pushed through door, some tossed out) finally crowd pushes in the door, cops go crazy, shots ring out, bodies fall, ambulance & sirens, A big black blanket is put over all.
All are become ocean, ocean rises.
Tides flush in & out. City appears.
Ocean destroys city.

Faust: when the ocean overcomes the living & takes away its blessings to destroy its children & they the incompetent children who furthered the course of destruction with their lives & fulfilled the horror of their incompetence are now themselves destroyed.

step by step directions

brightly colored paper mache masses are operated by brightly colored puppeteers

a) *several fall & get-up dances*
b) *mass chorale during moon entrance*
c) *string orchestra accompanies moon location changes*
d) *masses take away instruments from orchestra*
e) *sun set-up*
f) *agent 1 directs police in channelings of masses*
g) *agent 2 pulls individuals from masses*
h) *masses line up in front of door*
i) *several admissions*
j) *several toss-outs*

HISTORY OF LIGHT

Our birth and sculptor our maker and grandmother light grandmother of day construction worker of the human architecture of its face, eater & provider, drinker and nurturer, she who makes the dawning of our sustenance, by our littleness, by our work, she our light & our light's mother, finds the dirt for the modeling, models the dirt. You day may you succeed, you day may you be accurate.

Then the light didn't go anywhere, it just stayed & didn't move. This was the peopling of the face of the earth, they came into being, they multiplied & the light made them drunk, they had daughters, they had sons, but there was nothing in their hearts, nothing in their minds. They just went wherever they wanted to. They did not grasp the light, they did not understand it, so they accomplished nothing. They became the first numerous people on the face of the earth. And the lights office issued a humiliation & a demolition.

They were made of dirt & the dirt was killed when the sky devised a flood for them. They were not competent & so they were killed, done in by the flood. Their faces were smashed because they were incompetent. The earth was blackened because of this & the black rainstorm began all day & all night. Everything spoke to them. Their knives & their spoons, their cooking pots & their water jars. Into their houses came the animals small & great. Their pigs & chickens told them: you caused us pain, you ate us, now it is you whom we shall eat. This is the service we gave you when you were still people, but today you will learn of our power. We shall grind your flesh, their grinding stones told them. And this is what their dogs said: We don't talk. So we have received nothing from you. How could you not have known. You did know that we were wasting away there behind you. And their cooking pots spoke to them; pain, that's all you have done for us, by setting us on the fire you burn us, now we shall burn you. The stones, their hearthstones were shooting right out of the fire, going for their heads. Now they run for it, helter-skelter into the fermented light. They want to climb up on the houses, but they fall as the houses collapse. They want to climb up the trees, they're thrown off by the trees. They want to get inside caves but the caves slam shut in their faces & the light runs away from them. Such was the scattering of the human work, the human design. As the light withdrew its power the people were ground down, overthrown, the mouths & faces of all of them were destroyed & crushed by the absence of light.

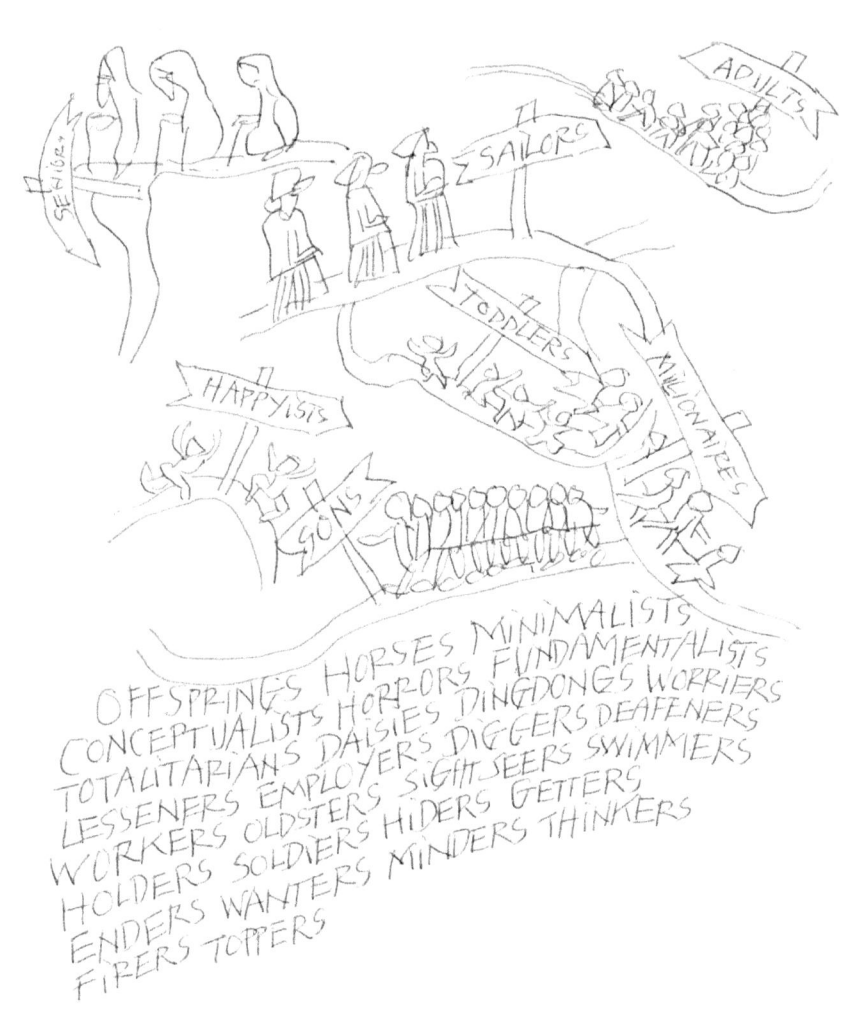

FAUST3 SLOGANS & WISECRACKS

1

the forest has never been wiser & less inhabited, full of its secondary wonderment & so distant from its recreational purpose & frightening to the soul

2

7 billion ape-related gods

3

the moments that are made to speak address the undressed wounds of the whole

4

you, the owner & inhabitant of the day at hand are obliged to reign supreme & re-invent the exhausted order of the day

Scene 3

COCKROACHES

Faust & accomplices point out life on city ruins with the help of large canvases.

Post-city life features:
- a) *Dogs, worms, cockroaches*
- b) *Bodycarriers*
- c) *Fancy characters perform simultaneous dialogue scenes: kitchen, bedroom, parlor, office, each with its own plot, consisting of conflict, solution, work, unemployment, health problem, deskwork, vacation, each scene 2x.*

Scene 3 (simultaneous scenes)

a)   Kitchen

Suppertime, not yet, give me 5 minutes, can you set the table, no, yes, serving spoons please, please watch, this is hot, can you pass the salt, what's this, it's good, yes, very good, can we have dessert, not yet, who'll do the dishes

b)   Bedroom

My hand fell asleep, can you rub it, more? Yes more

c)   Parlor

The economy is what it is, the economy doesn't like us, why we do what we do, isn't part of the deal, there is hardly any breathing space, why, because of the bills, the bills are what's called the economy

Parlor 2

You? No, or you, no, or somebody else, that's not likely, excellent, what do you think, me? Ya, oh, I think, anyway, the assumption is that it's all or nothing, nevertheless, it won't hurt to try, why not? Exactly, in the meantime things develop in unexpected ways, but the facts aren't in yet, & when they are nobody is sure, when they are we'll make our decision known, that's more or less what I was trying to say & while we aren't sure we might as well relax, exactly, I'm sure I will, ok, mostly that's all we can do now, undoubtedly, ok.

d) *Office*

Our job is to respond as forcefully as possible even to minor needs, we have to shift our strategies endlessly in response to the whimsy of these minor needs, why are we doing this, this question goes beyond our duty and capability, just realize: if we stop we get a lot of folks in trouble.

directions

post city dancers perform 4 new-life dances
- a) cliché kitchen dance
- b) cliché bedroom dance
- c) cliché parlor dance
- d) cliché office dance

(either 1x or 2x)

<u>the authorities</u>

proletariat 1: we don't make enough
proletariat 2: to pay rent

proletariat 1: rent

proletariat 2: that's a serious problem

upper echelon: NO

proletariat 1: why

upper echelon: it's obvious

proletariat 1: how come

upper echelon: you guys

proletariat 1: rent

upper echelon: are you kidding me

proletariat 2: no that's exactly what it is

upper echelon: my god, you guys. Listen to yourselves. You think that's what life is all about?

proletariat 1: exactly

proletariat 2: what do you mean, life

upper echelon: exactly, life

proletariat 1: life, step one: pay the rent

upper echelon: indeed, now you are equating the universe with your silly rent problem

proletariat 2: silliness isn't on our mind

proletariat 1: we are serious

upper echelon: Ya, that's pitiful

proletariat 1: O.K. Pitiful

proletariat 2: that's what is pitiful.

upper echelon: can't you pick something big like famine or war to complain about but that shitty little rent

proletariat 1: that's the problem it's not little

upper echelon: in the face of all the problems all over

proletariat 2: this is problem #1

upper echelon: Jesum

proletariat 1: and has nothing to do with Jesum

middle class: I lost my middle class job & now I am a lower middle

class unemployee and I agree, life is ok or not ok but the rent is definitely not o.k.
upper echelon: you guys are all sick you can't see the forest for all the trees.
proletariat 1: our trees are about to be chopped down
proletariat 2: I can't pay my student debt.
upper echelon: take a class in money making
proletariat 1: where
upper echelon: over there
proletariat 1 + 2: OK let's go
Money teacher: what's your desire
proletariat 1 + 2 + middle class: how to make money.
Money teacher: well there are 3 categories of money making a) legal (slow) b) illegal (fast) c) extralegal (not as fast). The chief element of success in any of the categories is planning. The making of a plan itself as a creative process is a satisfying step towards the desired end effect: satisfaction.
Faust 3: At this point we have to interrupt the class. The subject matter contains discrete information, not meant for the public's ear. Thank you, gentleman
Money teacher: You're welcome.
proletariat 1: my grandma can't pay for the pills she needs, do you have classes for getting my grandma her pills
upper echelon: that's not the problem
proletariat 2: what is?
upper echelon: the problem is, we aren't strong enough
mob: (very loud)
upper echelon: we need to be strong again
mob: (very loud)
upper echelon: our defense system is weak, we need much more sophisticated fighter bombers that can do the job.

mob: (very loud)

super christian: the lord says the righteous will be rewarded

mob: (loud)

the authorities: Yes, ladies & gentleman, we the authorities fully support and enforce the lord's opinion about righteousness

proletariat 1: but what about us, the proletariat?

upper echelon: the proletariat doesn't exist anymore.

proletariat 2: that's what I thought: we don't exist.

upper echelon: this is a democracy

proletariat 1: what do you mean

upper echelon: you have the right to be poor, rich or whatever you can afford.

Authorities: this is a problem we are fully aware of and we are working very hard to study the root causes of this problem.

Faust 3: That's enough. Thank you very much.

Scene 4

THE BANQUET

The essential chef, also featuring: customers, sous-chefs, fishmongers, onion distributors, culinary-institute observers & health dept. officers.

Chef: We can do it. The purpose of this particular meal is to satisfy all opposite forms of hunger, hunger which results from malnutrition or poverty or hunger which results unaccountably from the vast excesses of global overproduction & food overdiversification & is usually not recognized as such.

The essential chef: One tablespoon of pepper over here, thank you, & now as we start this historic meal, we raise our glasses & propose our first toast to the anonymous produce delivery truck driver, father of 4 barely knows his kids' names, sacrifices his life for diversity food delivery, but is earmarked for hell, because of family neglect – but on the other hand, if hell does not exist anymore, as the latest hellscience strongly suggests (not all international data are collected yet) – he may be applying for heaven & that we are told in culinary circles is a real & realistic possibility for food transportation personnel. A toast to the anonymous lady or gentleman! Prosit! The first chapter of heaven manifests itself in better work legislation, shorter hours & weeks, longer vacation, etc. & the 2nd chapter is extralegal access to superlative & even supernatural forms of satisfaction in unlimited quantities as typical for eternity procedures.

Individuals who qualify for this advanced stage of fulfillment line up over there at door N° 2, where samples of futuristic & overt happiness are demonstrated and taught.

And now dig in & enjoy the meal!

(Banquet)

step-by-step directions
a) *large table is set up*
b) *elegant waiters set dishes & decorations*
c) *dancers with signs: guest 1, guest 2 etc. repeat essential chef sentences + gestures*
d) *glasses, attached to fishlines fly off table during toast*
e) *fulfillment applicants line up at door, are admitted + checked out*
f) *fulfillment exercises*

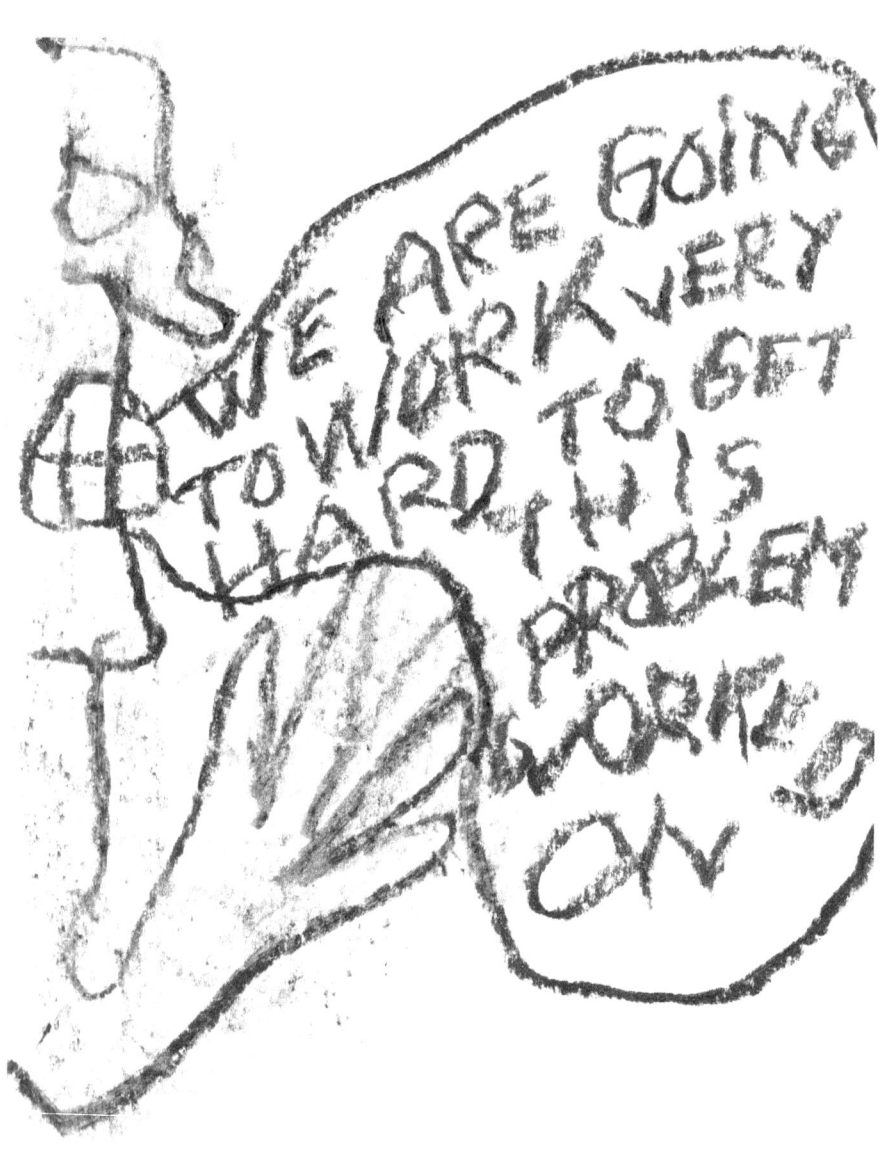

5

even the most neglected lumber roads, turned into mudhavens,
contribute to the majestic reign of the crowned giants,
the superb windwhistlers

6

applicants beware, you can only apply for the whole thing,
nothing less

7

up & down haven't happened yet & the extremes of up & down in
your brain have not materialized & have not resulted in the violent
upheaval that was needed to overthrow the shallow definitions which
describe up & down

8

to reign supreme you must be as bright & yellow as a daffodil &
cannot afford any lesser brightness

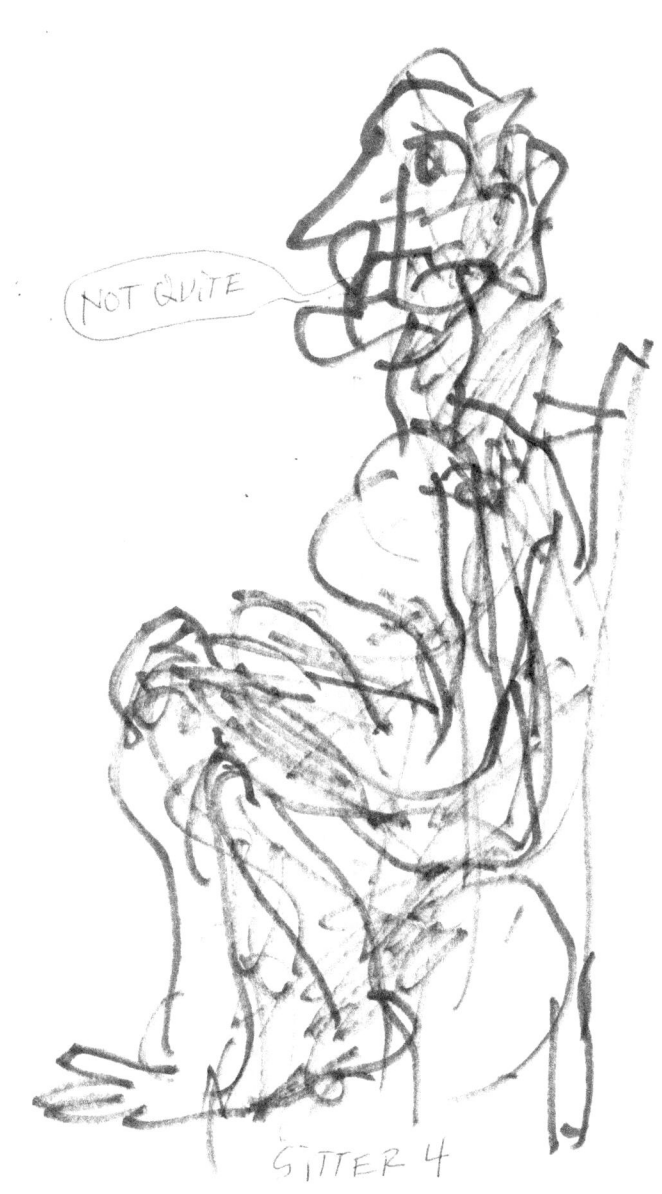

Scene 5

THE SITTERS

Distress artists demonstrate chaos of refugeedom: a) tossing clothes at them, then thunderstorm to drive them away from clothes, b) organizing waiting positions & fast reactions to unexpected aggression, c) show example of animal migration, d) language school, teach basic phrases.

Words must be omitted because the refugees' distress is in the chaos of fast evasive movements & sudden imprisonments which descriptive words cannot convey: the unbearable, including all the dangers but none of the grace of animal migrations.

The sitters are the concerned impotent researchers of the crisis, endlessly analyzing cause & effect, but locked into their chairs & selfhoods as into the culture which they represent. The religion of pity which they uphold can only help as far as pity can help, but disaster's reality is too complex for pity.

SITTERS' JOBS

1) STATIONARY STILLS

2) changing location

5) encatching the problem

6) falling / setting up

4) dancing upsetness

3) tremblings

7) eating + drinking during clients

Sitters' jobs:
1) *stationary stills*
2) *changing locations*
3) *tremblings*
4) *dancing upsetness dances*
5) *lining up & encircling the problem*
6) *falling & getting up*
7) *eating and drinking during disaster*
    a) *single chair attendance 5x*
    b) *single file*
    c) *auditorium*
    d) *chaos*
    e) *quick group moves*
    f) *the chairs are equipped with pull strings. When a refugee crowd moves towards the chairs, the chairs back away.*
    g) *An animal herd migration is demonstrated*
    h) *herd destroys chairs*

Forever, not so much, ah, maybe, not quite, over there, yes, there there there, ah, maybe, all the way, maybe, forget about it, go, not yet, no, not yet, I said not yet, you, really?, really, let's go, alright, why, because, all the way, if not us it's someone else, they don't know, no, if they would, they might, if they would, this whole thing could happen, yes, what's up, yes what, this whole thing could fall apart, it's too much, maybe, who knows, but if they would we might be in it, well, yes, all kinds of things happen, well, who knows, it's always the same, really?, really, you think you might just drop it, yes I might, on the other hand, when you think of it, yes, I agree, let's just go, no no no no, ah

SITTER 10

BOOTS

Boots traversing landscapes. Landscapes succumbing to boots at regular intervals. To amplified stomping sound followed by long low reverberation horn chorus. The landscapes are painted canvasses that get crumpled & tossed under the boots.

Scene 6

THE GENERIC NERVOUSNESS

The populations of the planet are rounded up for inspection & evaluation. Angels are used to corral them into appropriate formations. The hands & eyes of old gods are mounted high above them to assure them of some vague divine security. The main characteristic of the populations is their generic nervousness in respect to their basic rights & guarantees for more than an animal life, e.g. to not eat each other, even though killing each other is not illegitimate in the larger order of things, where any extraordinary experimentations with law, order & justice are easily overruled by the larger reasons for war.

The sitters who are definitely deeply affected by their pity-religion are nevertheless unable to argue against these larger war-producing reasons. Finally, in the absence of any perceivable solution, Mother Death is invoked & asked to address the total situation.

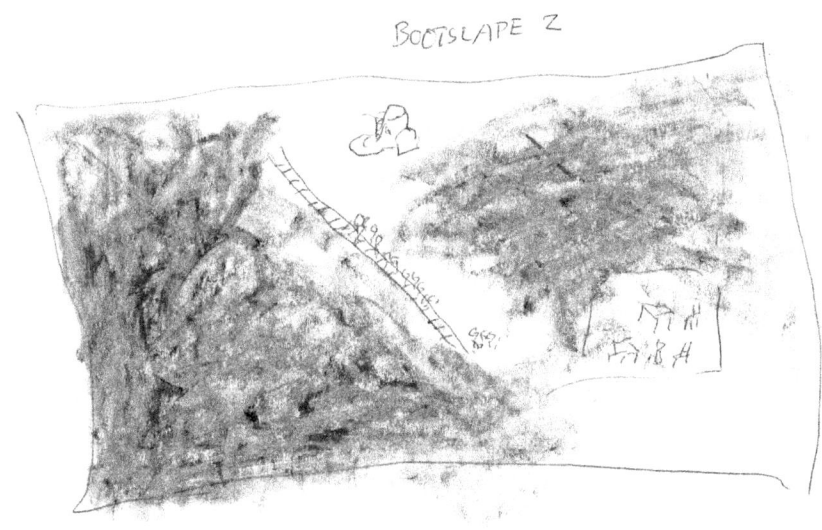

Scene 7

PLANETARY DANCING

She who is married to Life itself, declines to appear in person but sends a delegation. The religions which have all tried & failed with all their musclepower to eliminate the above-mentioned conflicts are now going onto their knees in acknowledgment of the Death delegation. The delegation is announced prominently, arrives, silences all noises & arguments & starts its work: disordering the existing order. All populations are instructed in both practical & esoteric ways in the methodology of disordering the existing order.

The ensuing chaos shows no population-caused bloodshed, is generally peaceful & slowly & surely accelerates all normal human mingling moves into post-cultural forms of planetary dancing (the instructors are Lubberland nationals)

a) noisy dance of death
b) death delegation in silence
c) 3 examples of disordering the existing order of life
   i. day & night
   ii. high & low
   iii. more & less
d) Lubberland dance instructors give planetary dance lesson accompanied by marshmallow orchestra

FAUST3 SLOGANS & WISECRACKS

9

only the forest can cure the lost souls who stumble into its
dark opposite, opposite the human fortress

10

neither economical nor spiritual well-being are a sufficient lure
for the life-deprived detailers & organizers of allocated time

11

we who are what we are & not the same as the divine majority
who lives by persuasions that make it other than what it is

12

doers are doors opened to the extreme clashes
between exterior & interior

Scene 8

SUCCESS SEEKERS

Success seekers, minimum wage citizens, prisoners, organists, christians, gun advocates, gardeners, wall builders, itching teenagers, political prisoners, taxi drivers, seers, balancing artists, falling artists, lumberjacks, billionaires, media customers, food stamp collectors, actors, non-actors, mothers, grandmothers, gods, priests, post office clerks, tenants, apple orchard farmers, sheep farmers, math professors, nuthatches, lawnmowers, dentists, dogs, emergency nurses, sopranos, architects, marathon runners, cancer patients, tree pruners, mountaintop removal engineers, fiddlers, dwarves, totalitarians, seniors, soldiers, lost souls, kids

3 ENGINEERS

THE GOING GOING GOING GOING GOING GOING GOING

LIGHT AUTHORITY

FAUST & HIS SECRET AGENTS
HARD AT WORK TO DISMANTEL
ONE THING OR ANOTHER

Scene 9

MARCH OF THE TREES

The march of the trees forward & down the hills is the revolutionary march that yearns for victory over the planetary destruction strategies of its overbearing inhabitants. Tree marches are not registering with human offices, they are as secret as they are revolutionary. Puppeteers are in charge & have themselves trouble to understand them sufficiently for proper execution of the upwards – forwards – inwards & outwards that the trees request. Local population members fall down amongst the trees & pick themselves up again & again to exercise the uprising muscles that planetary revolution needs.

All other activities surrounding these marches must be suspended for maximal impact of the prescribed one-directional flow. Flags may spring up like spring brooks in wild spurts to emphasize the importance of the moment in time. Silence must reign during the event till all of a sudden the revolution explodes in percussive frenzy, unstoppable.

- a) *alternating tree movements & hill movements*
- b) *overbearing inhabitants capitulation ceremony*
- c) *a fast flag event*
- d) *violent cymbal concert*

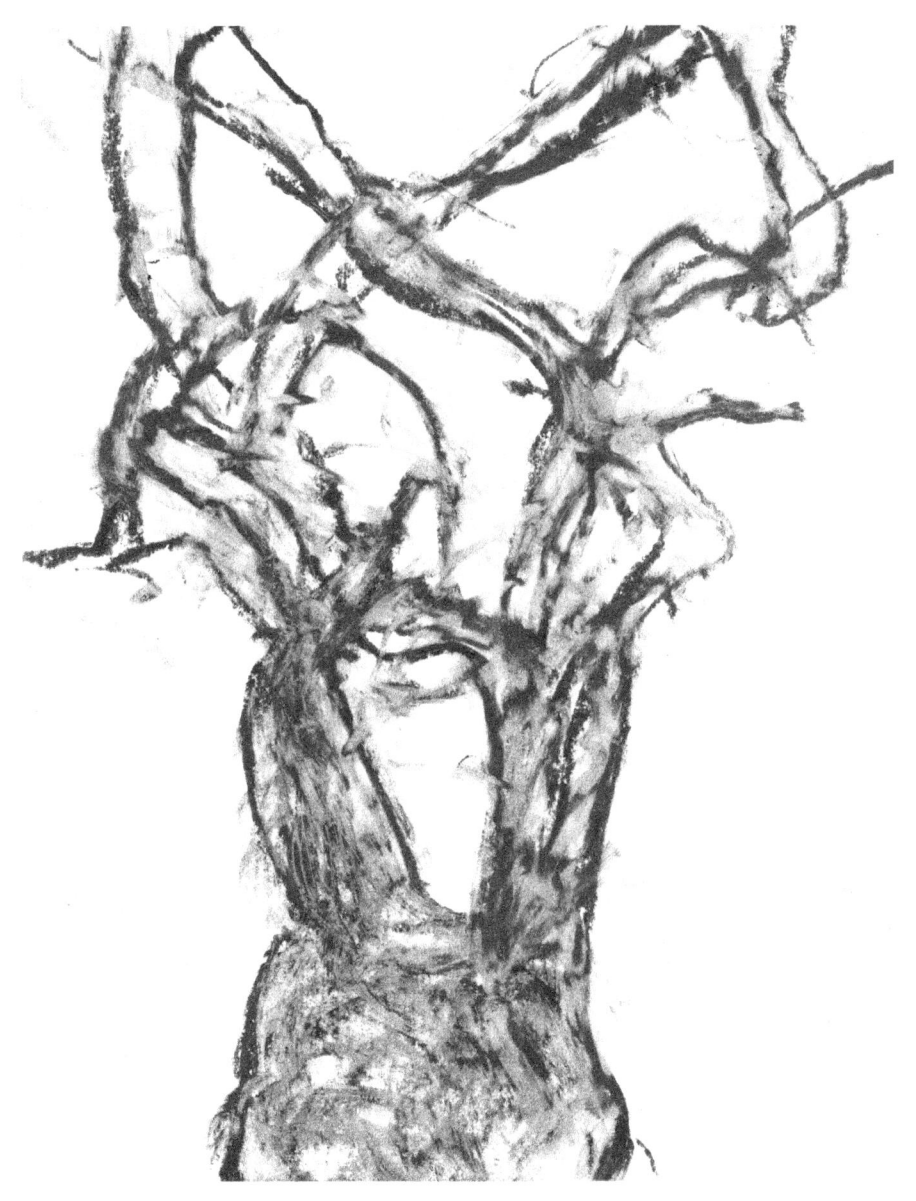

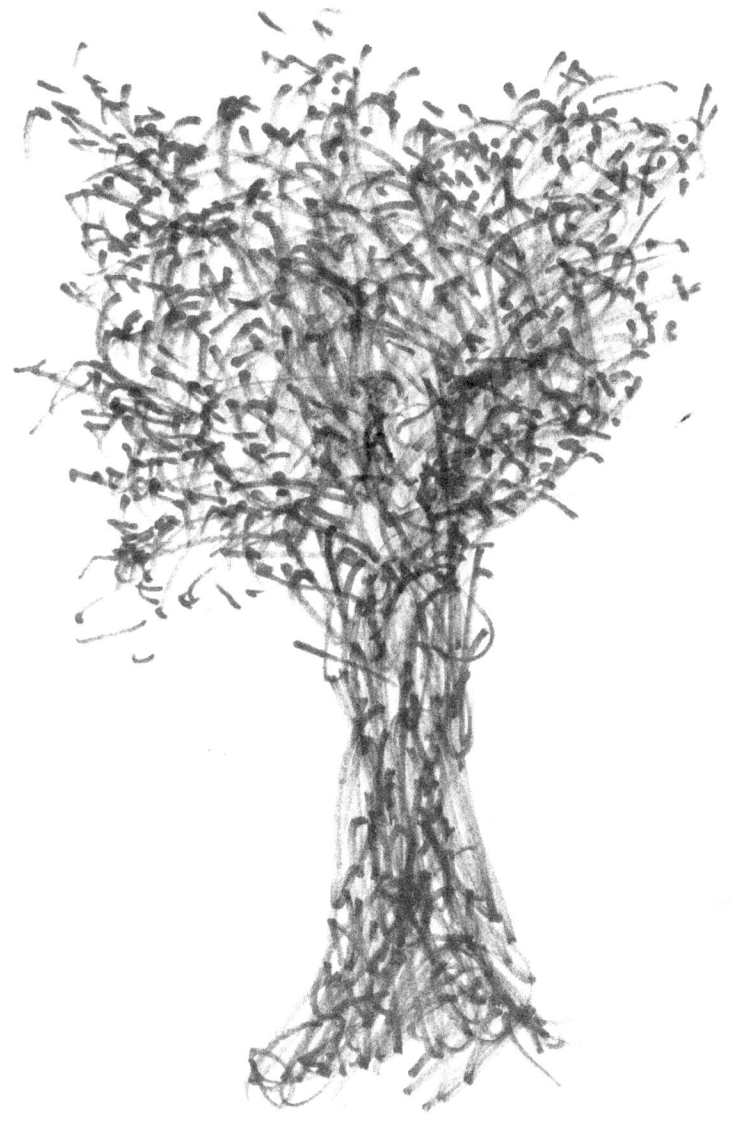

Scene 10

FAUST 3 DANCE CLASS

The twittering of the chickadees requires action from the listeners & I don't mean the cat who wants to jump them. It requires all creatures to behave accordingly, noisefully, flightfully to take off from the burdensome slow ordinariness & wiggle your life away, senselessly, joyfully because of the sun's majestic presence which instills powerful reactions in your bones & your torso. Because that's our predicament: to use our wings & hop up & down as good we can to correspond to the day's warmth & existence. Nothing more, nothing less.

For this precise reason I now announce Faust 3 dance classes that specialize exactly in those chickadee imitation moves.

13

the nobility of martyrs, saint or terrorist, shines its light
on the irregular causes which further the good & the bad

14

the thoughts think the edges of the unthinkable & get their
muscles from that exercise

15

the rain that showers us is the dissolution of heaven that hugs us

16

continuation is unlikely unless it makes itself felt before it is needed

Scene 11

FACTORY

The factory has the packers. The packers are hard at work packing the unfinished things that the factory provides. The factory piles up the things. The things are not yet the result. The result results from the things being packed up. The packers are in charge of finishing the unfinished result. The result is the precondition for the continuation. The things have to become a result & the result needs packing up, to insure continuation. Only continuation can claim to be the final product which connects the future with the present & which allows the packers to make a living & then to live in consequence of making a living.

- a) wrapping & unwrapping repeats
- b) 2 oversize puppets paraded: the future & the present
- c) demonstration of living in consequence of making a living
- d) organ fugue as superfluous death puppet is attached and dismantled by packers

WE THE STREAM
PERSUADE THE
WILD TERRITORIES
TO DIRECT THEIR
LIFE

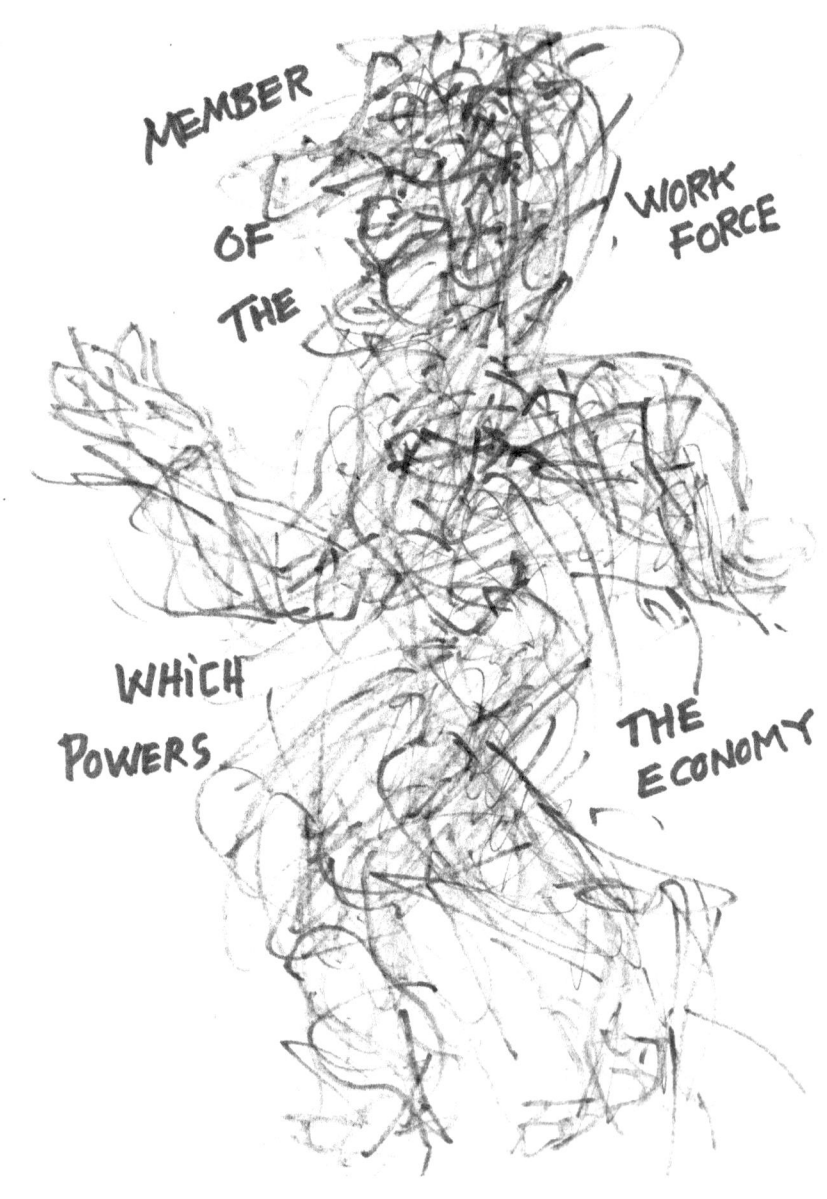

Scene 12

FAUST 3 SPEECH TO HIS ACCOMPLICES

We, when we are a stream, flood the outlying territories. The territories are lying there, not knowing what for till we flood them. When we, the stream, flood the territories, the territories awaken from their unknowing sleep, as they hear the organ fugue which emits from the stream. The awakened territories are dangerous like colts & wild boars. The awakened life inside the territories makes them wild like boars. We, the stream, persuade the wild territories to direct their life which was awakened by the organ fugue against the death that has settled in, because the death which has settled in is not the same as the death which is law, but is a superfluous death, whom the territories must defeat with their life which was awakened by the organ fugue.

Scene 13

THE GUN

The unrecognized organize to design bang-bang work, in order to produce decisions. The bang-bang decisions need workers, who emerge from speaking to the unrecognized. The bang-bang work is the death-giving work of the unrecognized. The hollows inside creation are essential to the death-giving workers, as they fill the hollows of creation with arbitrary quantities. The quantities are from the participating life. The bang-bang work eliminates arbitrary quantities of life which participates. The participators don't know the workers or their why. The why lives inside the unrecognized. The why does not appear in the analysis of the participators. The secret why inside the unrecognized is the secret. Quantities of participators are lost to the secret. The proliferation of the secret is from the everyday bang-bang proliferation.

 a) *gun preachers & politicians & merchants advertise practice & ownership of guns*
 b) *the unrecognized get job as death workers*
 c) *scythes, representing guns, mow down crowds*
 d) *US arms sales oratorio, based on latest statistics*

THE HOLLOWS
INSIDE CREATION
ARE ESSENTIAL
TO THE BANG BANG
WORK

FAUST3 SLOGANS & WISECRACKS

17
the crucified human animal hangs next to the crucified human spirit who claims saviorship & eternity amidst peasants with shitty lives. His unalleviated pain matches the injustices of peasant life. The indoctrinated imagination of salvation equals the death wish of the sufferer. The imagination cannot admit that there is no salvation

18
nothing missing, everything is here, except the here

19
substance emerges unexpectedly from the expected

20
brightening, a result of fading light

Scene 14

THE SPECTACLE

The king is the authority that creates the reason for the spectacle & then hires the force that conceives of it. The king needs to be elevated from the average to the appropriate height for supervising the spectacle. The hired force which produces the elements which make the spectacle, engages the drama that ordinary life hides in itself & rearranges its ingredients into the spectacle, as supervised by the king who hired the force. The spectacle has to emphasize the importances. The importances are extralegal occurrences that have so far failed to impress themselves on the public. The public needs to be clothed extraordinarily for the occasion of the spectacle. The spectacle can only take place when all proper preparations are made, including dress code compliance. The dress code enforcement task force briefs the public on the occurrences to be expected in the ensuing drama to prevent improper overreactions by the un-initiated. The spectacle can only take place in the presence of the initiated public, supervised by the king.

- a) *king elevated to appropriate height*
- b) *ordinary life actors are hired*
- c) *audience is assisted to dress for the occasion*
- d) *king administers initiation rite*
- e) *(murder dumbshow)*

BOOTSCAPE 7

BOOTSCAPE 8

Scene 15

BATTLE 1

As the combatants fall or are sickened by battle the strugglers take over to do the combatants' work, not only fighting the obvious, which needs their fight, but replacing the confused battleground of the passionately wrong with pastures where guns are words and tanks are sentences. Defeats happen on the pastures & the defeated are raised by grazing animals & incarcerated by the sky that was absent from their life before the battle.

- a) as combatants fall, strugglers retrieve their weapons
- b) stick dance
- c) cows raise dead combatants
- d) skypainting wrapped around combatants

Scene 16

BATTLE 2

Combatants' devastation slaughter mayhem machineparts sticks & garbage mixed with torsos hands heads all elements collected not for burial but for re-employment in the transformation of combat zones into battlegrounds for the causes of wounded life & life stripped naked & need rearranging for newly invented battles – or are strapped to horsebacks to speed up the process. Wounded life & its messages are taken to the foreground to be exposed to the public & the public is inspired to extract garbage & weapons from the combat zone for re-employment in empty lots & gardens. Wounded life gardens employ arms & legs harvested from combat zones till growth occurs.

a) *skypainting removed from field of torsos arms legs hands & hardware*
b) *singular items shown to public with musical accompaniment*
c) *hands & feet strapped to horseback*
d) *gardeners attach hands & feet to ploughs*
e) *musical ploughing*
f) *potatoes harvested*

BATTLE 2

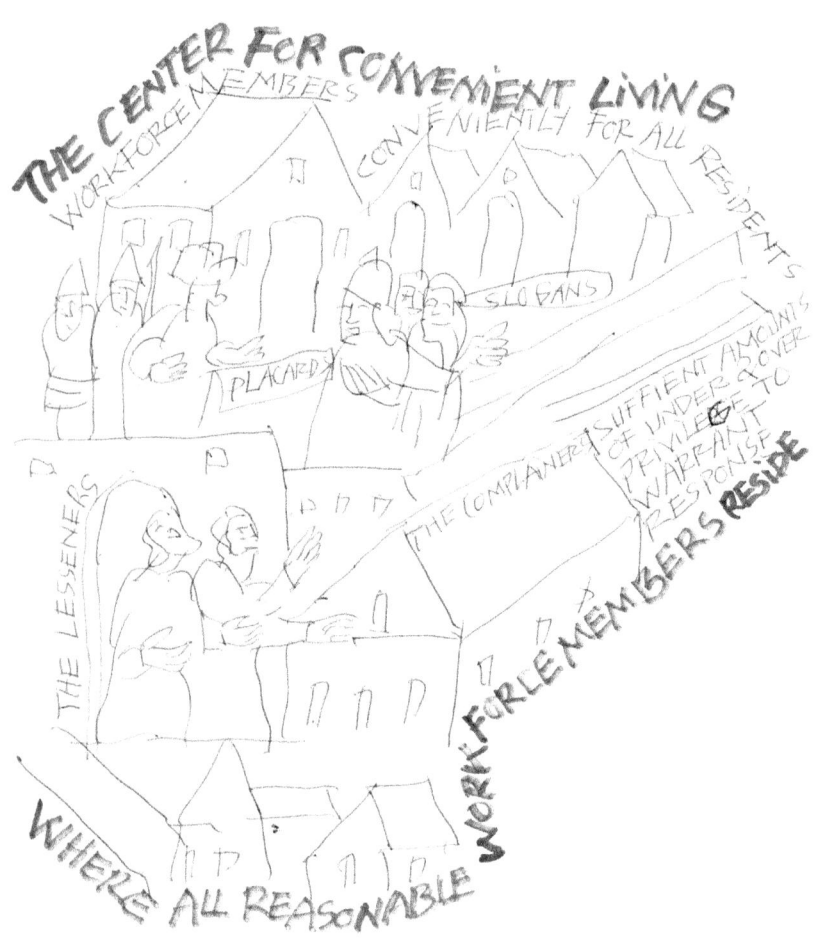

Scene 17

THE CENTER FOR CONVENIENT HISTORY

The offices of complainers & lesseners located conveniently for all residents in the center for convenient living where all reasonable workforce members reside. The complainers file their complaints & then wait diligently for the office's response. The lesseners are there with placards & slogans addressing the problems of abundance & over-productivity – both groups represent sufficient amounts of under- & over-privilege to warrant response from the office. But the office is an historic site, the clerks themselves are historians who are able to put even the most recent misgivings into historical perspective, which means: the miniscule changes that result from the parties' advocacy are pre-ordained to strengthen the center's traditional system.

    a)   *complainers with slogans parade*
    b)   *lesseners with slogans parade*
    c)   *officers process all slogans politely*
    d)   *an o.k. hymn is sung*

21

the good is the apple tree's magnificence

22

the good is the ewe's call for the lamb on its way to the slaughterhouse

23

the good is the courage of the scream against the bad

24

the good puts light into the dark day's soup

CRUMBLING CITY DURING SUN
ADORATION SERVICE

Scene 18

SUN ADORATION SERVICES

You can't be not here when the sun is here. The sun holds you & promotes your being, nails you down where you are or drives you on to where you are not. The moment is not yours, it's the sun's.

All other demons that urge you this way & that way are minor powers & are easily as related to the sun as you are. All your posturings & lock-ups into your individual concentration for questionable outcomes are nevertheless warmed by the same warmth & would benefit from the plain & simple adoration services that the sun requires.

    a)   *sunpuppet with large feet walks over prostrated bodies & raises them*
    b)   *circle dance around sunpuppet ending in a thank-you bow*

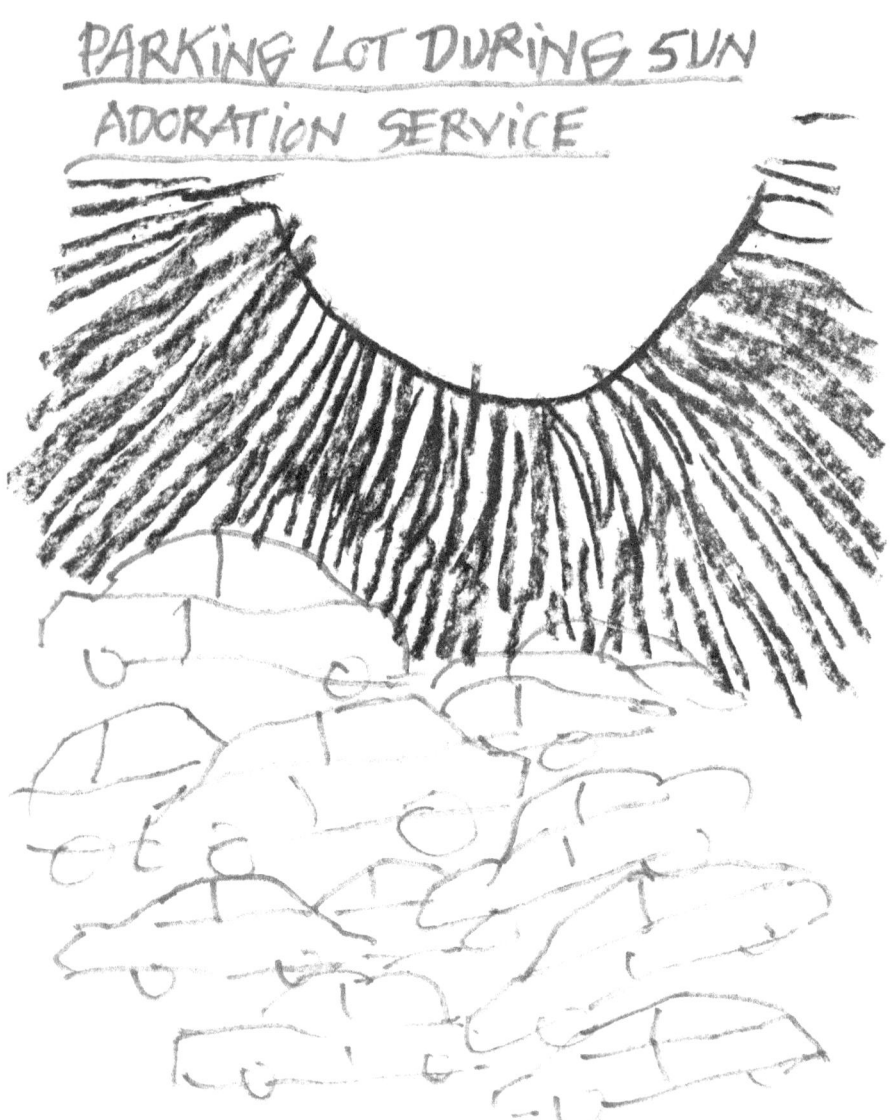

SUN ADORATION SERVICE OFFICER

OLD COUPLE DURING SUN ADORATION SERVICE

Scene 19

DIAGONAL MASSES

The walking of the masses, interrupted only by off & on individual breaks always continues diagonally across the cities & into the surrounding countryside. The masses need to walk as directed by their own feet over & through the thicknesses which their own labor has massed up in front of them. They need to traverse & overcome what they themselves have created. The preachers & sermonizers who try to redirect them fail to influence the anarchic flow. Gods, usurpers, demons & profiteers instill their passions in them but cannot change the urgent flow that obeys only its own momentum. All migrations, all flights of refugees, hunger, war & pestilence are walking in this unending walk that contests the ocean's ebbs & floods & resembles the rivers, that start modestly as brooks high up in the mountain & by collecting all neighboring brooks on their path become mighty streams rushing to their unknown destination.

a) papermache crowd walks through & over cardboard city repeatedly
b) text 19 is recited in fragments, bringing the walking of the masses to a halt

THE REFUGEES PROTEST
REFUGEEDOM AS THEY
FLEE
A RIVER GOD THROWS
HIS JUNK AT THEM
CLOUDS BURST
FLAMES SURROUND
THEM
THE TASKFORCE "FATE"
BEATS THEM UP
NURSES NURSE THEM
& ARE BEATEN
DRONES KILL
THEM REPEATEDLY
UP AGAIN

SITTERS' DANCES & GESTURES INTERSPERSED
SOMETIMES MORE SITTERS THAN REFUGEES

Scene 20

THE WALL

a)   Wallbuilding team hired by the executives of the wallfaith congregation: this is it, it's there & once it's there you make it stick, & once it sticks they'll believe in it even if they hate it.
b)   Walldestruction team: this makes excellent material for the cellars of the mushroom growing enterprise, pile it over here, easy access for the dump truck, yes, alright, a little more to the left, correct.

The wall is built by landscape transformation. The green of the hills & the clouds of the sky are turned around, erected, painted & stuck up high as a monument for everyone to see, beast are corralled, human crowds are driven by the sheer force of their suffering to run their heads into the wall. Wallarchitect & wallvictims alike secretly know that the wall is the landscape that formerly housed & nourished its inhabitants. Wallarchitects & wallvictims alike are gifted with hands that build or destroy the wall.

Disobedient hands break away from their bodies & exercise their right & restore the landscape that the wall deprived them of.

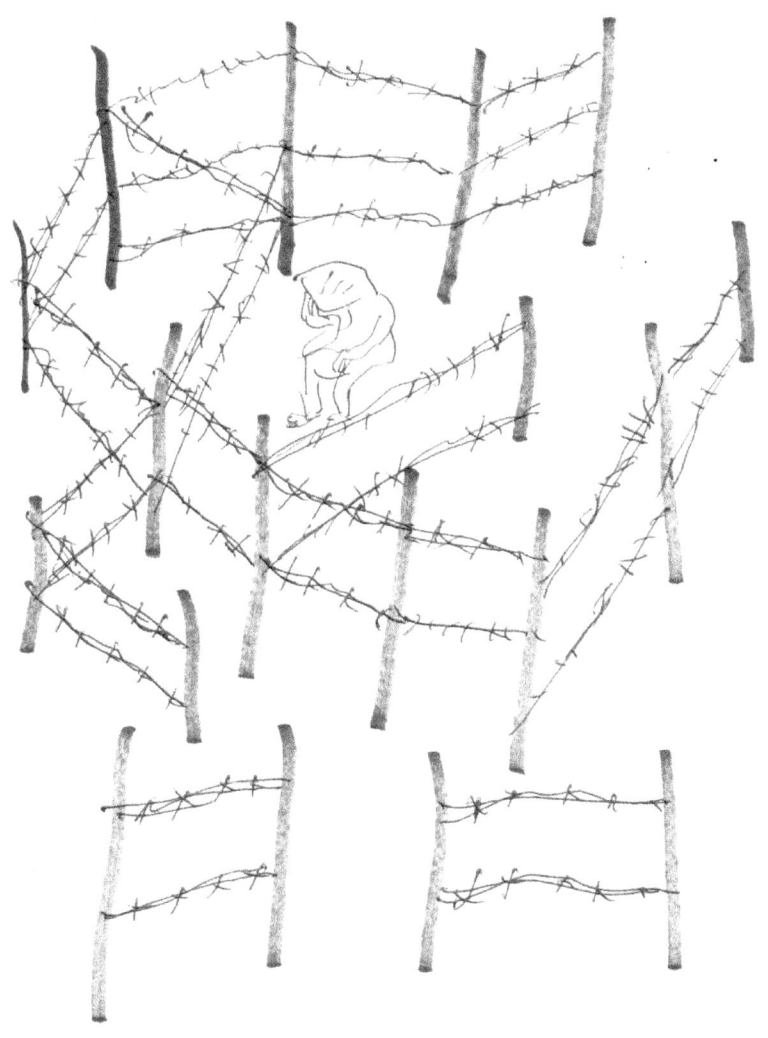

25
god is a misspelling of good

26
the good is phenomenal not logical

27
the office of imminent rainstorm issues the yellow that smashes the evening gray

28
solutions are not asked for, rather indiscriminate uncertainties that contain solution & failure

Scene 21

VICTORY SYMPHONY

When the seers arrive the foot-draggers are obliged to organize their randomness into sense, sense means the sense of living more than the inherited life had in mind. The living includes all necessary aloofness & all manner of flight attempts even fake ones whose failure is already in the design.

Combat ends in truncated bodies, not victory: victory is the privilege of the battleground in which no truncating happens. Victory is the name of the altar that demonstrates the state of living other than the inherited life. Victory is the name of the roaring brook & the flow of real & massive justice. Victory orchestras are battleground orchestras which reconstruct the noises & notes of the past into the real & necessary music moment in now-time. Victory musics are unprivate unpsychological forwardmoving masses of sound that include crazy sounds made by crazy instruments.

    a)   *roaring brook victory altar constructed from naked papermache bodies*
    b)   *roaring brook victory orchestra performs*

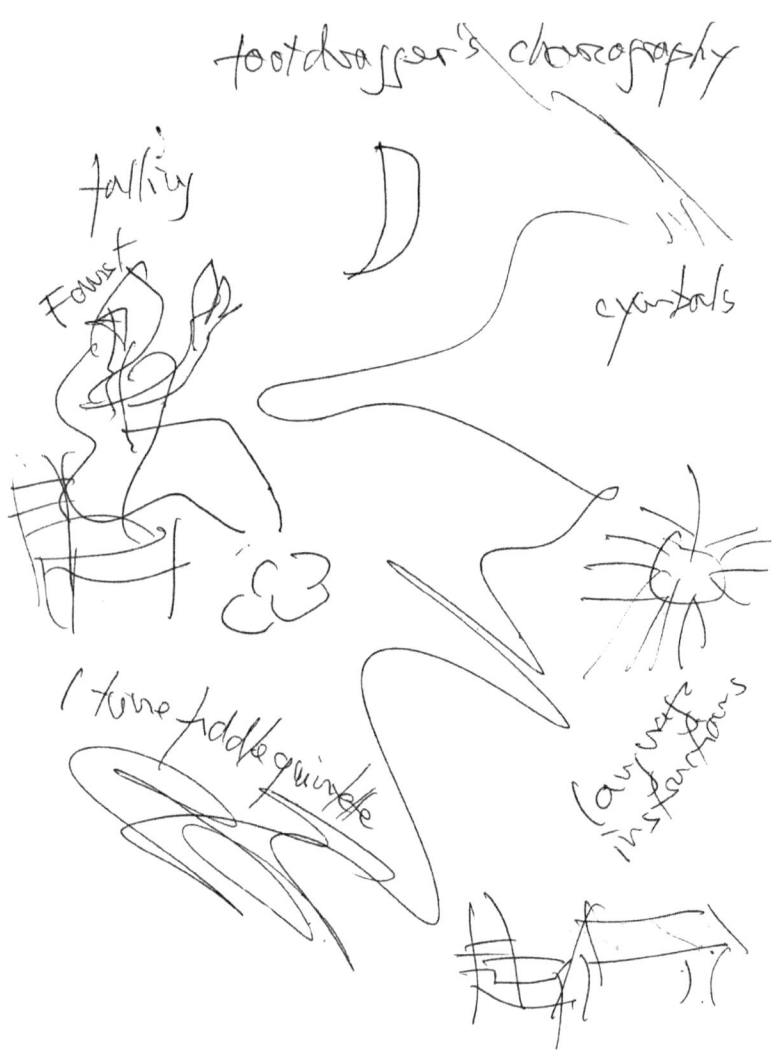

Scene 22

ANTI-HISTORY DANCING

What thinking marches are coming from the dancers who want more than marching steps, what rhythms that upset the destruction specialists of history. Marching which continues history must be upset by marches that disrupt history & direct themselves willfully against consequential history. The this way & that way marches are joined to produce snakelines, swirls & circles that embrace the spaces in which they take place, what falls gets picked up, what stumbles is utilized in arhythmical stumbling progressions. Arms which propel the torso in support of leg swings are initiating new swinging moves that inspire hops and leaps. Meadows & roads can be filled with the throbbing flow of participating bodies in the ebb & flood of the human mass uprising.

a) *goose-stepping soldier march*
b) *transformed into hop-hop-hop dance by Lubberland dance instructors*

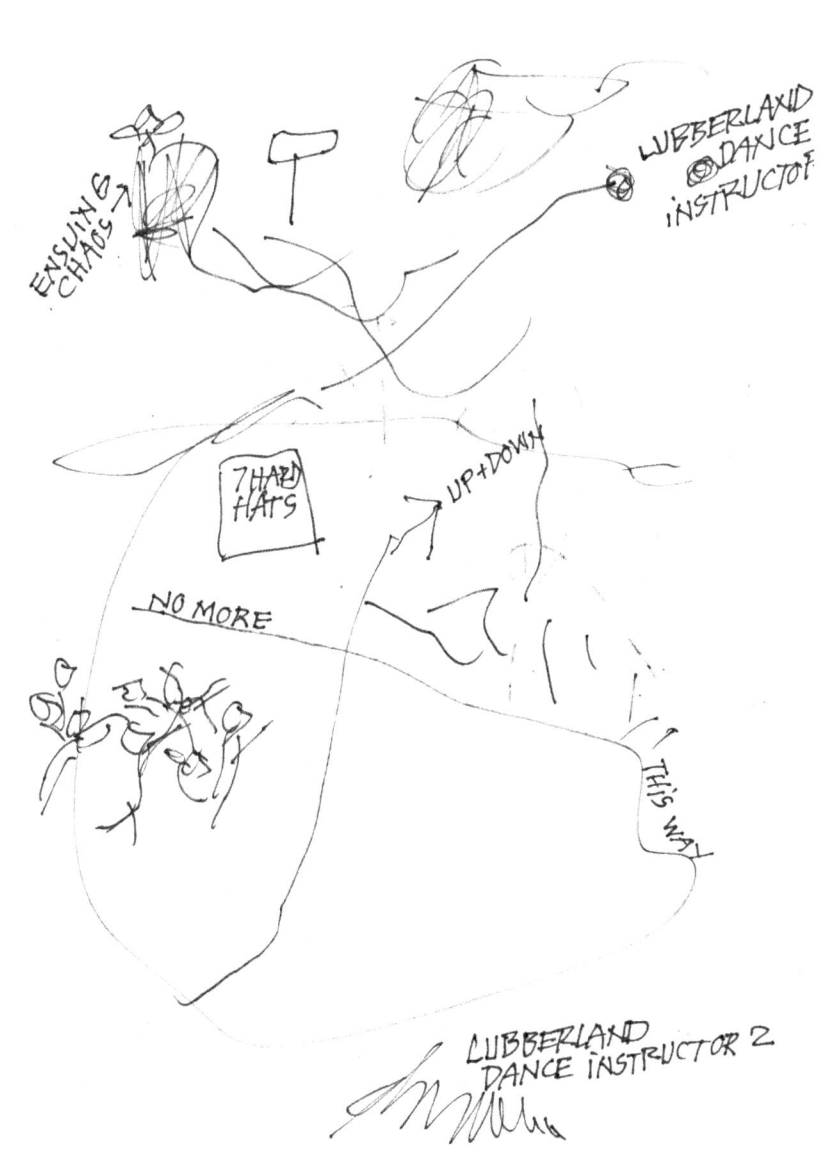

Scene 23

THE DAYKEEPER

The down & up of the day's forenoon & afternoon. The day's strength of embrace as well as power to toss its customers into little abysses of unknowns or the urge to recruit its very own army to defeat the undaylike obstacles.

The sitters who decide on the day's direction, but are unable to control its upheavals. The single day's universe & uncompromising demands which require a full understanding of its beginning & the gifts that are hidden in its beginning. The human adjustment to the day's animal likeness. The need to instigate pauses for reassessment into the day's hurry.

Children and grandchildren of the day, who are invisibly there in its every minute & whose function is to extract the futuristic elements from its fated proceedings.

Grandmother of day, daykeeper addresses the day: you day may you succeed, may you be accurate, may you accomplish what the light allows.

A HISTORY-OF-LIGHT EVENT

a) moving & rattling of chairs
b) dressing animal body over chairs
c) address of the daykeeper

Scene 24

THE DEED

deed: a thing consciously done

The deeds are presented & overemphasized for the sake of literature & historic record. Ordinary or repetitive deeds are not registered. Art is engaged to glorify the individuality of deeds. Consequently hero worship & religion are instituted & the parading of deeds is made a necessary byproduct of the state's functioning & posturing. Deed competition is a major part of the education system. Deed hardware & military arsenal are major aspects of the economy. Musicians take deeds away from their contexts. Dancers & gesturers bypass the production of deeds. Undone deeds overwhelm the doers.

a) *deed-ammunition-factory produces context*
b) *musicians & gesturers bypass context*
c) *factory workforce re-employed by musicians & gesturers*

29
life-lessening inventiveness

30
nothing trembles as much as the whole

31
time making & squandering in magnificent unessentials

32
the nature & beneficial characteristics of collapse contradicted by the sun's inevitable victories over necessary & unnecessary darknesses

Scene 25

THE OFFICE

All activities are registered in the office. All humans are applicants. All applicants submit to the history which created the office. All officers of the office are recruited from the current economy which sustains the living. All applicants are stripped of their arbitrariness & are made members of the workforce which powers the economy. All activities are meticulously assessed & selected by the office to construct the achievement which the economy needs for its services. All services are of equal importance. All importances are joined & fastened into place till the desired satisfaction is produced.

    a) *all applicants in picture perfect pose for the start of the race to the desired satisfaction*
    b) *importances fastened into place*
    c) *text 25 recited by spectacular costumes*

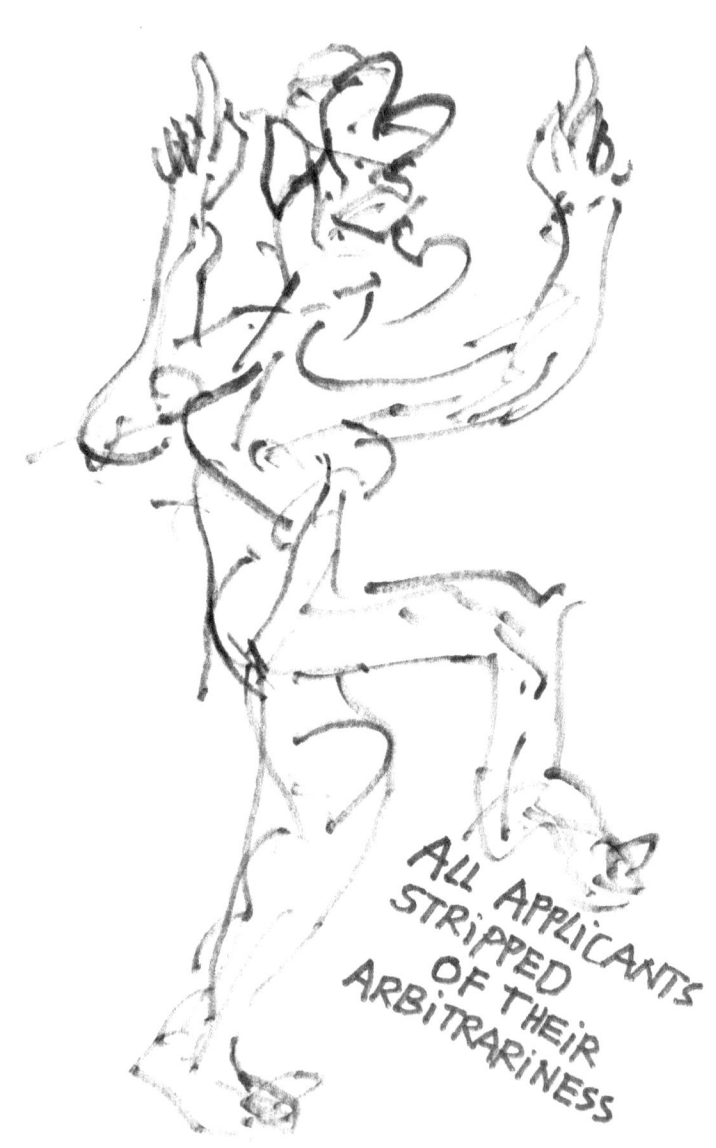

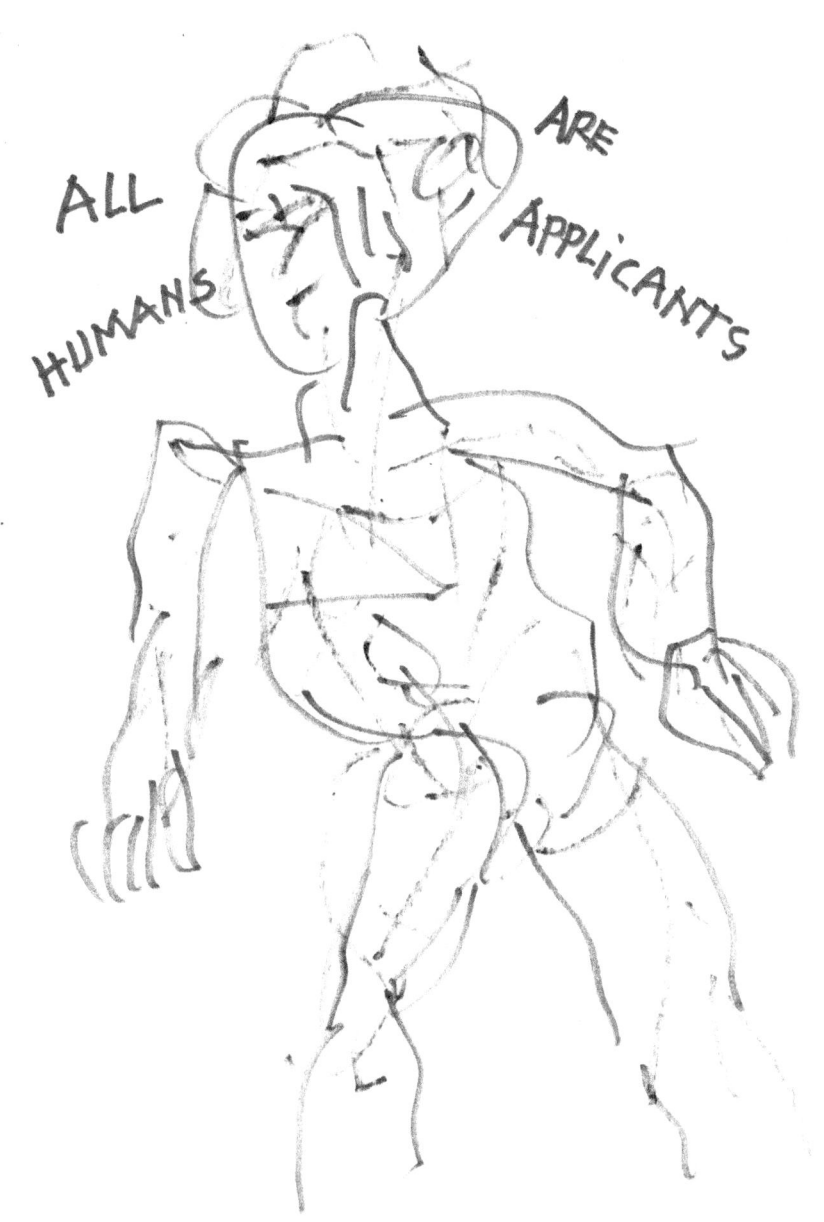

Scene 26

THE CEREMONY OF THE THINGS
Carrrying, holding, placing, putting, bringing, giving, setting down, receiving, running, mounting, pointing out, admiring, employing, unemploying, putting away with the help of guardians, explainers, pointers, keepers, registrars & secretaries. Stone, cup, branch, sand, dirt, paper, can, shoe, pot, spoon, hammer, chair, window, scissors, glasses, book, shirt, sock, coat, hat, saw, pillow, sheet, box, bucket, shovel, broom, pen.

Singers, dancers, gesturers in a variety of costumes, become the handlers of the things.
1) *They wash and dry their hands.*
2) *They pour lightbulb light over their hands.*
3) *They open the eyes of a blindfolded oversized face & show it a thing.*
4) *The things get carried & put down.*
5) *The things get wrapped and carried again.*
6) *The things get unwrapped & put away.*
   Each thing gets its varied procedure, including a musical performance.
7) *The final move is a circular passage from one handler to the next*
8) *The thing is paraded.*
9) *Then celestial objects: moon, stars, suns & clouds are set up to preside over a large table on which the things are placed.*
10) *Skeletons and soldiers are ordered into destruction positions.*
11) *Preparations for the execution of the things include percussion set-up & placement of garbage bin or coffin.*

12) Detailed police whistle commands progressively facilitate the destruction & funeralization of the things.
13) At the peak of the aggression, at the precise moment when destruction is imminent, the celestial bodies get agitated, their hands taken from them & applied to dismantle the guns, scythes & other weapons.
14) A musical celebration follows.

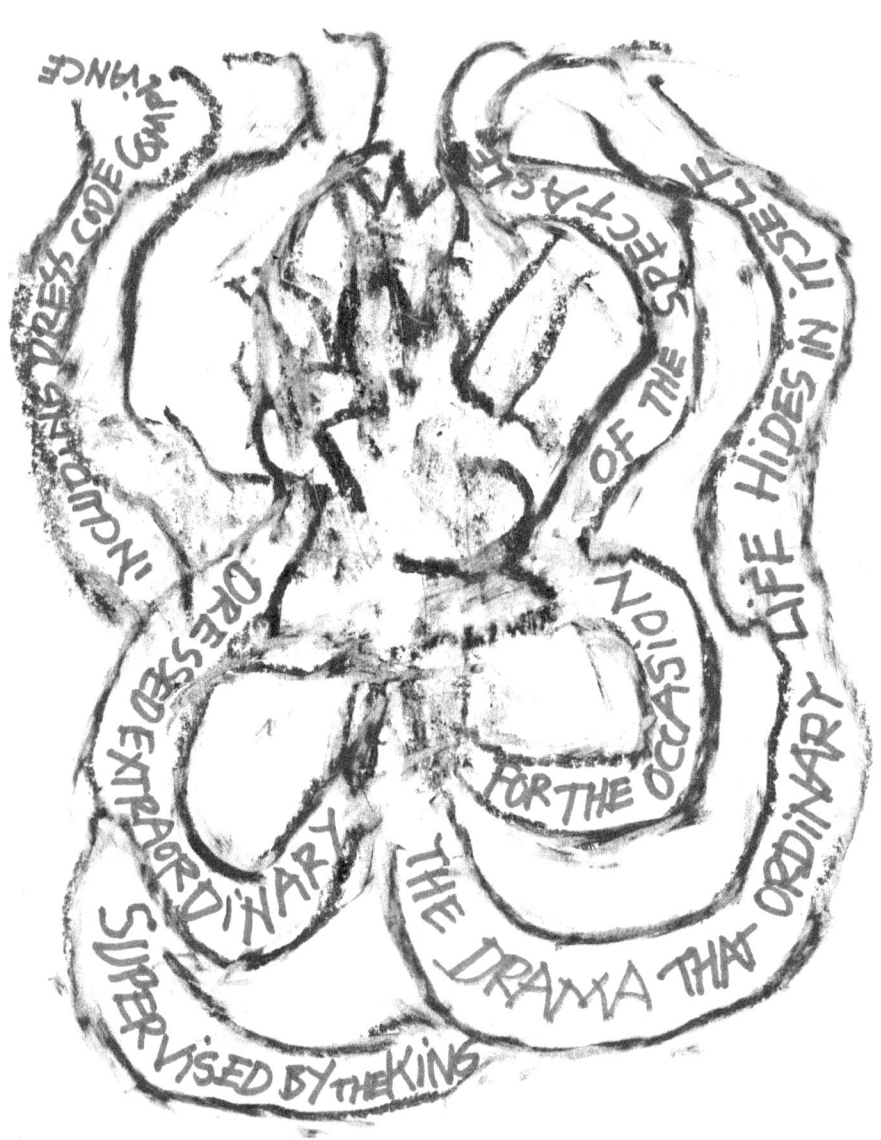

FAUST'S SLOGANS & WISECRACKS

33

our work not work but a leap in the air & an admission of our divine origin

34

hunters, butchers, soldiers, murderers kill time because time is life

35

the dust rises against the economic supremacy because it's the dust of the earth, the biggest small thing that the market can't possess driven by the storm that the future brews in its innards

36

we chirpers & ranters, unfit for anything more serious than chirping & ranting, can't ever get enough of it

BOOTSCAPE 7

BOOTSCAPE 8

Scene 27

MR. & MRS. NOBODY

Faust 3 and his agents work hard on erecting a scaffold that keeps collapsing.

Mr. & Mrs. Nobody first watch, then laugh, then call in the laughing choir.

They conduct the laughing choir as Faust 3 agents keep trying & failing.

BOOTSCAPE 9

BOOTSCAPE 10

37

the wind-orchestrated afternoon hour is the precise eternity that ecstasy invents

38

meanings in their original stage are confused & therefore become the appropriate tool for tackling confusion

39

you, the owner & inhabitant of the day at hand, are obliged to reign supreme & re-invent the exhausted order of the day

40

to reign supreme you must be as bright & yellow as a daffodil & cannot afford any lesser brightness

Scene 28

FOREVER

trucker, tycoon, seniors, innocents

I'm driving through the dark no question about it. Our gray shadows are now black. It's so dark. It's so dark nobody can hear me. We are providing light across the board, that's our job. You? What the sun can't do, where he can't reach, that's our job. My feet are stuck in the mud, I don't get anywhere & there is no light at the end of the tunnel. Access yourself of the available services. Which ones? What we call light is a business trajectory with advisory capability. I just want to sit in that bar & pour a couple of beers on my depression. We are walking up & down & to & fro on the same path going nowhere. Yes, in almost total darkness. Ladies & gentlemen, please understand: light is our business, we are here for you. We are working on schedule. Our goal is to make light accessible to every one of you. Every one of you deserves light. We are working hard to provide for you the adequate quantities. Our profits prove that the scheme is working. Light is at the heart of our enterprise. I am cold. My life is dark. These black clouds over there don't seem to move anywhere.

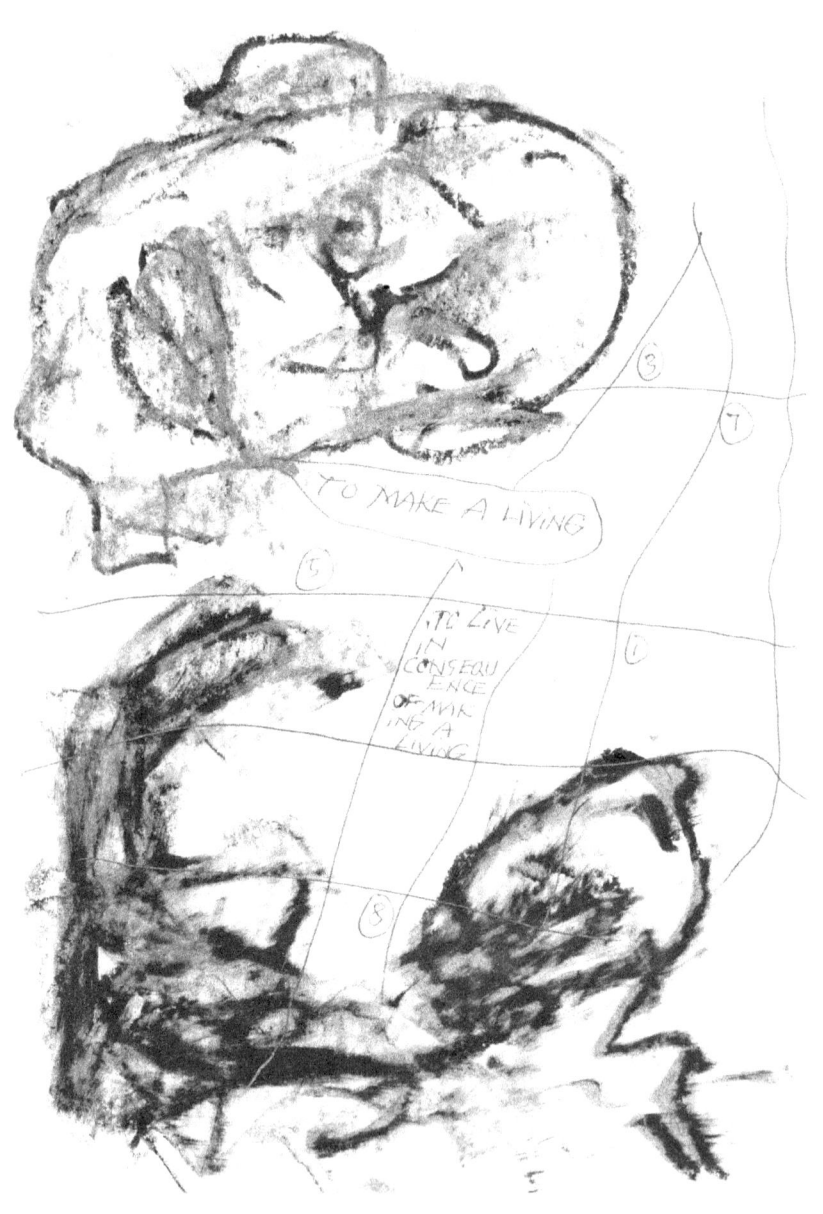

Scene 29

WORK & UNWORK

Work is what you do, not why or what for. Work means: paving the road to the luxury hotel where the beneficiaries reside. Work is the screw that holds the whole thing together. The whole is the mysterious result of material history. The result doesn't have you in mind, it means itself – a mystery-self that rarely ever gets photographed. You work to make a living, the living means rent & food, not life. Life is something else. The discussion of life cannot take place under making-a-living conditions.

Unwork grows potatoes & generally specializes in cheap habits to sustain the not-making-a-living. Unworkers are creators, whereas workers are active contributors to the existing order of life.

Product is born from work. Product is a circular fact that derives from the making-a-living non-life & aims for refuse. Refuse is the consequence of product & aims to reproduce product from the raw material refuse. Excellent product is excellent obedience to the making-a-living non-life. Excellence is well-functioning absence of life.

a) a professor of work demonstrates work's characteristics with the help of model worker
b) a professor of unwork demonstrates unwork with the help of garden tools

FAUST3 SLOGANS & WISECRACKS

41

meaning is constructed from the debris of the everything wanting to be something

42

the thoughts that compose a person will also decompose that person

.

43

once you decide to be a tree, your body bends to the wind & you listen with the ears of the superb musicians that inhabit you

.

44

the light is homeless

Scene 30

YES-YES & NO-NO CHORUS

The unrelenting pursuit of property as sure-fire path to happiness. Since you can't own yourself because at least 1/3 of it is owned by the hospital you entrust it to, you have to look outside the self to achieve ownership & its logical conclusion, happiness. The economics of the political system to which you belong encourage & advantage ownership over all other human qualities & help you fight the bothersome restrictions that keep you from quantitatively superior access. The educative tools for property enhancement, car, home, family & the endless gimmicks of the information industry lead you to the indiscriminate growth you need for happiness production. And once you get to the 1st step, you easily advance to step 2, 3 & 4 till your total 2/3 self is entirely surrounded, encrusted & magnificently elevated by property which finally appears to be able to hold death at bay (according to the latest statistics).

Scene 31

FREEDOM

The incarcerated mind has nothing but freedom in mind, freedom which is an election campaign slogan & is a US privilege of the advantaged over the disadvantaged. And even the sweetest Republican freedom does not include freedom from the Pentagon but rather the freedom to maximize freedom-smashing Pentagons. Therefore freedom fighters come in such diverse categories: correct ideology fighters, wrong-population-in-the-wrong-place fighters, etc. The incarcerated mind lacks the basic freedom to think, because thinking is an educated convenience in an incarcerated landscape – landscape, a non-commercial term for real estate is incarcerated exactly because of its usefulness & has a hard time existing outside its usefulness.

directions:

during text recital animal herds & flocks of birds migrate, are hunted & harvested repeatedly

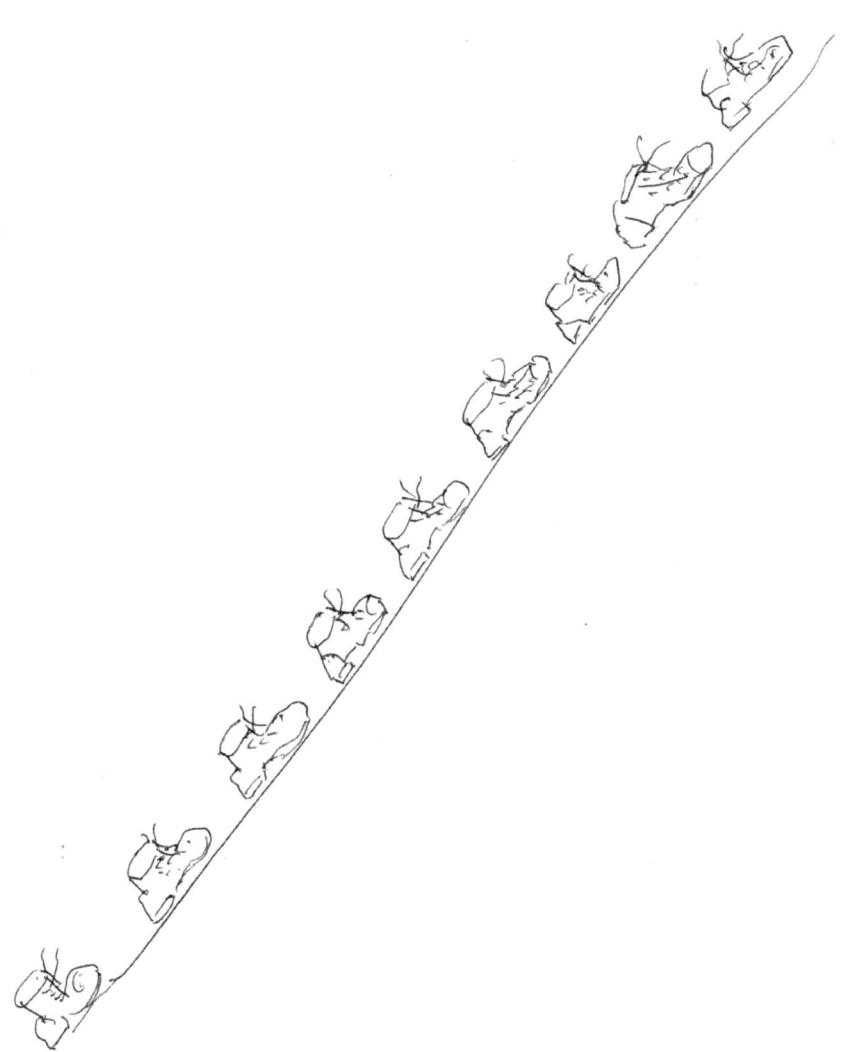

Scene 32

EDUCATED HIKING

The top-of-the-mountain idea derives from the low-landers who can't see enough. The hike to the top promises an eye-opening that the physical strain of hiking guarantees. The hikers' thinking is educated by the education system that guarantees satisfaction. The hikers know already what they will see. The vast panorama of the expecting mind is the actual, material promised land, minus one or two dreams. Because the hikers during that strenuous hike know already the picture-perfect outcome, the education system from which they graduated bears the burden of deciding the details of the picture-perfect totality of the promise.

Most hikers soon realize the scam & give up climbing. Most educators of the system are aware of the scam. But the inbred magnetism of the promise pulls throngs of hikers towards the steep mountainside, never mind the falling & crushing on the rocks.

Hand puppets are used to show climbing & falling from steep mountainside

BOOTSCAPE 11

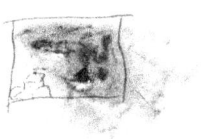

Thank yous

Donna Bister & Marc Estrin for design, editing & general advice, Esteli Kitchen & Josh Krugman for diligent electronic transmissions, & my grandson Ira Karp for his inspired scribbles into my notebook which I transformed into some of the drawings.

Fomite

A fomite is a medium capable of transmitting infectious organisms from one individual to another.

"The activity of art is based on the capacity of people to be infected by the feelings of others." Tolstoy, *What Is Art?*

Writing a review on Amazon, Good Reads, Shelfari, Library Thing or other social media sites for readers will help the progress of independent publishing. To submit a review, go to the book page on any of the sites and follow the links for reviews. Books from independent presses rely on reader to reader communications.

For more information or to order any of our books, visit
http://www.fomitepress.com/FOMITE/Our_Books.html

More Titles from Fomite...

Joshua Amses — *Raven or Crow*
Joshua Amses — *The Moment Before an Injury*
Jaysinh Birjepatel — *Nothing Beside Remains*
Jaysinh Birjepatel — *The Good Muslim of Jackson Heights*
Antonello Borra — *Alfabestiario*
Antonello Borra — *AlphaBetaBestiaro*
Jay Boyer — *Flight*
Mike Breiner — *The Way None of This Happened*
David Brizer — *Victor Rand*
Paula Closson Buck — *Summer on the Cold War Planet*
David Cavanagh — *Cycling in Plato's Cave*
Dan Chodorkoff — *Loisada*
Michael Cocchiarale — *Still Time*

Fomite

James Connolly — *Picking Up the Bodies*
Greg Delanty — *Loosestrife*
Catherine Zobal Dent — *Unfinished Stories of Girls*
Mason Drukman — *Drawing on Life*
J. C. Ellefson — *Foreign Tales of Exemplum and Woe*
Tina Escaja — *Free Fall/Caída libre*
Marc Estrin — *Speckled Vanities*
Zdravka Evtimova —*Carts and Other Stories*
Zdravka Evtimova — *Sinfonia Bulgarica*
Anna Faktorovich — *Improvisational Arguments*
John Michael Flynn — *Off to the Next Wherever*
Daniel Forbes *Derail This Train Wreck*
Derek Furr— *Semitones*
Derek Furr — *Suite for Three Voices*
Elizabeth Genovise — *Where There Are Two or More*
Stephen Goldberg — *Screwed and Other Play*
Barry Goldensohn — *The Hundred Yard Dash Man*
Barry Goldensohn — *The Listener Aspires to the Condition of Music*
R. L. Green — *When You Remember Deir Yassin*
Greg Guma — *Dons of Time*
Andrei Guriuanu — *Body of Work*
Richard Hawley — *The Three Lives of Jonathan Force*
Zeke Jarvis— *In A Family Way*
Ron Jacobs — *All the Sinners Saints*
Ron Jacobs — *Short Order Frame Up*
Ron Jacobs — *The Co-conspirator's Tale*
Scott Archer Jones — *A Rising Tide of People Swept Away*
Maggie Kast — *A Free, Unsullied Land*

Fomite

Darrell Kastin — *Shadowboxing With Bukowski*

Coleen Kearon — *Feminist on Fire*

Jan English Leary — *Thicker Than Blood*

Roger Lebovitz — *A Guide to the Western Slopes*

Diane Lefer — *Confessions of a Carnivore*

Rob Lenihan — *Born Speaking Lies*

Kate MaGill — *Roadworthy Creature, Roadworthy Craft*

Tony Magistrale — *Entanglements*

Michele Markarian — *Unborn Children of America*

Gary Miller — *Museum of the Americas*

Ilan Mochari — *Zinsky the Obscure*

Jennifer Anne Moses — *Visiting Hours*

Sherry Olson — *Four-Way Stop*

Martin Ott — *Interrogations*

Andy Potok — *My Father's Keeper*

Janice Miller Potter — *Meanwell*

Jack Pulaski — *Love's Labours*

Charles Rafferty — *Saturday Night at Magellan's*

Joseph D. Reich — *Connecting the Dots to Shangrila*

Joseph D. Reich — *The Hole That Runs Through Utopia*

Joseph D. Reich — *The Housing Market*

Joseph D. Reich — *The Derivation of Cowboys and Indians*

Kathryn Roberts — *Companion Plants*

Delia Bell Robinson — *Shirtwaist*

Robert Rosenberg — *Isles of the Blind*

Ron Savage — *What We Do For Love*

David Schein — *My Murder and Other Local News*

Peter Schumann — *Bread & Sentences*

Fomite

Peter Schumann — *Planet Kasper, Volumes One and Two*

Fred Skolnik — *Rafi's World*

Lynn Sloan — *Principles of Navigation*

L.E. Smith — *The Consequence of Gesture*

L.E. Smith — *Views Cost Extra*

L.E. Smith — *Travers' Inferno*

Bob Sommer — *A Great Fullness*

Scott T. Starbuck — *Industrial Oz*

Susan Thomas — *Among Angelic Orders*

Susan Thomas — *The Empty Notebook Interrogates Itsel*

Tom Walker — *Signed Confessions*

Sharon Webster — *Everyone Lives Here*

Susan V. Weiss —*My God, What Have We Done?*

Tony Whedon — *The Tres Riches Heures*

Tony Whedon — *The Falkland Quartet*

Peter M. Wheelwright — *As It Is On Earth*

Suzie Wizowaty —The Return of Jason Green

Silas Dent Zobal *The Inconveniece of the Wings*

www.ingramcontent.com/pod-product-compliance
Lightning Source LLC
Chambersburg PA
CBHW071618080526
44588CB00010B/1177